Cardboard & Paper-Maché Furniture

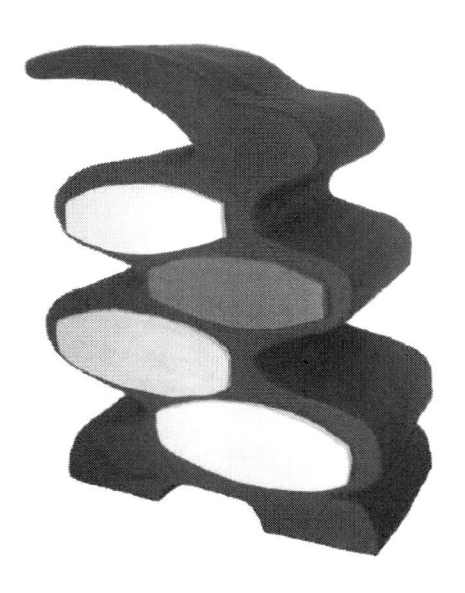

Riccardo Agostini

Cardboard and Paper Mâché Furniture

by
Riccardo Agostini

Dear readers,

You have an original book in your hands.
In addition to the technical explanations, more than 100 images will allow you to remember all the construction phases from the very beginning until you finish your piece of furniture.

Please start reading, follow my advice and you will build beautiful cardboard and paper mâché furniture, with just 20 steps.

The years I spent at the "Carnevale Aquesiano", making paper mâché masks and structures, have allowed me to refine and improve the technical realization of cardboard furniture. Combining cardboard and paper-mâché, I have managed to get structures of high quality and strength, which are able to support significant weights.

In this book you will find the most frequently asked questions I have been asked during my years of work. I invite you to take a look as you may find the answer to your questions!

What will I find in this book?
You will find detailed explanations, techniques, a list of tools, practical advice and examples to create beautiful furniture made of cardboard.

What do you offer us?
I offer you the opportunity of getting to know the tips and tricks needed to make unique pieces of furniture. With only few steps you will be able to design and build them yourself. I will explain how to obtain a robust design, what types of cutting tools are available and the related costs. In addition, you will discover how you can make waterproof and washable cardboard furniture.

Is cardboard-made furniture resistant?
Depending on the technique you decide to use, you can obtain resistant structures with a unique design. You can place a big television on the furniture or can even be seated on it without altering its structure at all.

Do I need to buy tools or equipment?
This manual will explain how to build furniture without the need of sophisticated equipment. There is only one element that you cannot miss: your imagination!

Do I need much space to make this type of furniture?
Cardboard furniture can be designed, assembled and painted at home.

Is painting easy to remove?
In case you get dirty when painting, the water colors can be easily removed using a damp cloth.

How long does it take to create a piece of furniture?
The time depends on the complexity of the design and the time devoted to it. In case of a small structure, like a bedside table, the time can vary between one to three weeks.

Is cardboard furniture durable?
The cardboard furniture is very durable. Its strength will depend on the technique and materials used. This manual contains the techniques that allowed me to get the best results.

Making this type of furniture could harm my children anyhow?
Only during the cutting phase, careful attention should be given by not having any children nearby to avoid any risk of getting cut with the cutting tools. Apart from this, each step can be done in the company of your children. All the used processes and materials are not hazardous to children's health.

Interlocking technique

At the moment of making a piece of furniture, you should choose the technique to operate. Today, the most common are the Interlocking (or honeycomb) and Layered techniques.

In these pages you will find all the information you need to master and achieve excellent results with the Interlocking technique. This method will allow you building lightweight, durable and quality furniture, while using a small amount of cardboard.

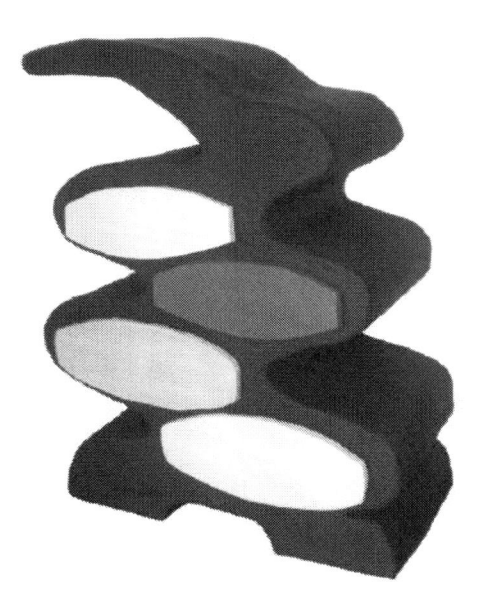

And here we go!

Design it

Take a sheet of paper and draw your furniture. The cardboard furniture, in contrast to the wooden made furniture, apart from being lighter, allows you to create any kind of shape even curved structures, so ... the limit is your imagination!

Example:

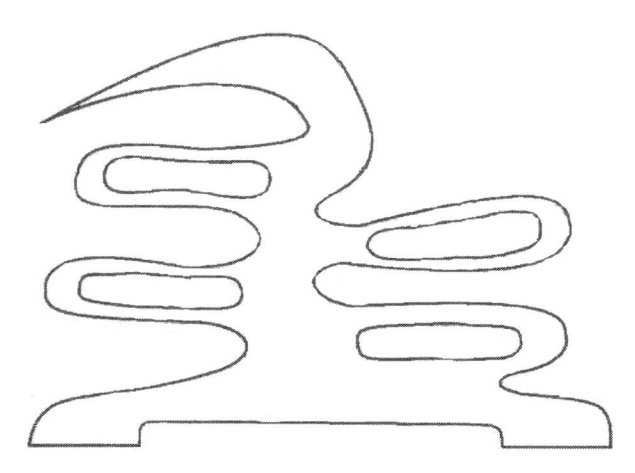

Plan it

Once your furniture design is ready, you need to determine its dimensions: H (Height), L (Length), P (Width)

Example as follows:
Furniture Dimensions H. 80cm, L. 55 cm, P. 30 cm

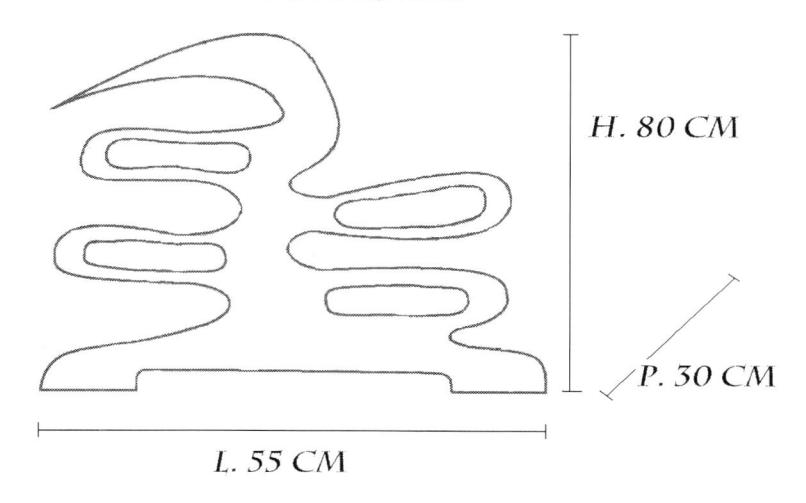

H. 80 CM

P. 30 CM

L. 55 CM

Material needed

- 8 sheets of cardboard 80cmx55cm, 1 cm thick

- Cardboard 0.5 cm thick

- 2 paper tapes of 2cm

- 1 cutter

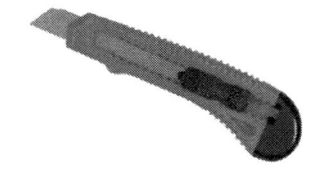

- 1 m. of sandpaper

- Wooden (or metallic) surface approximately 45 cm x 55 cm.

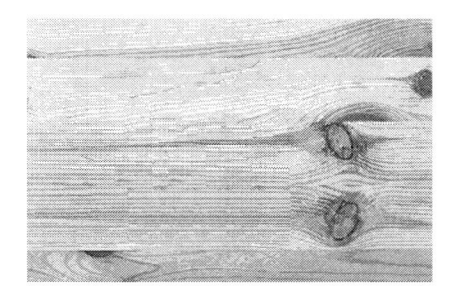

- Saucepan

- Newspapers. It is important to have a good amount of paper, making sure that blank and white and pink paper is available. Since several layers of paper are going to be applied, having newspaper with two different colors is recommended. In this way, it is easier to see where each layer has been applied. It is better not to use plastic paper because it does not absorb the glue and this could compromise the stability of the furniture.

- Setsquare

- Ruler

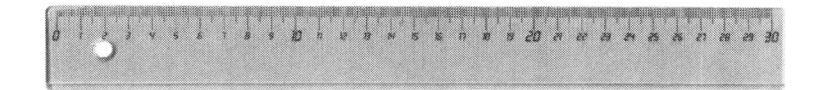

- Level

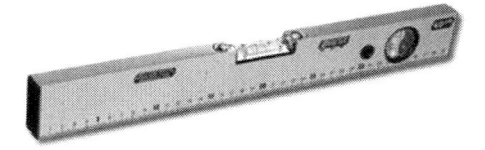

- Flour

- Whisk pastry

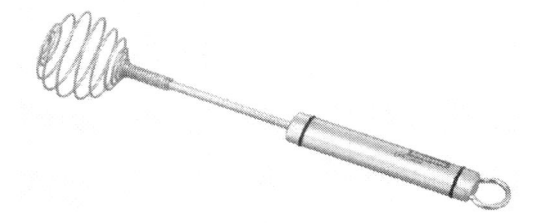

- 50 mm Brush

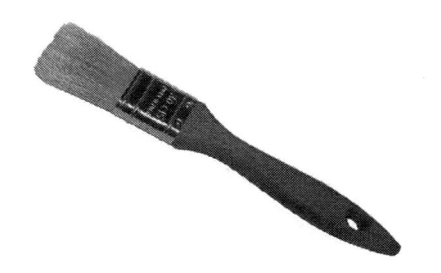

- Tape measure

- Pen

- Water based wood varnish

- Turpentine

Built it

Attention! From Step I to Step V, it is described how to convert scrap cardboard in sheets of 80cmx55cm, 1cm thick.
If you already have several sheets of cardboard 80x55 cm, 1 cm thick, you can continue reading from Step VII.

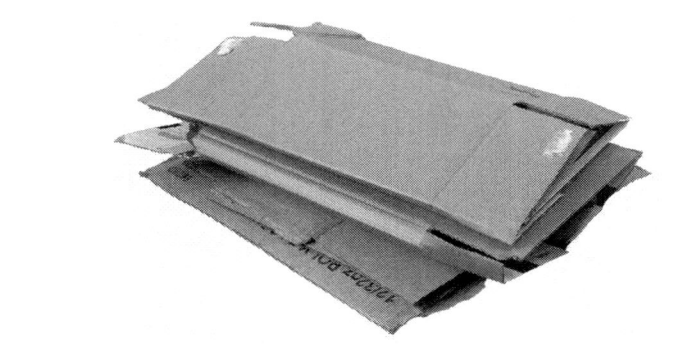

Fig. 1 - scrap cardboard

Fig. 2 – cardboard sheet (80 cm x 55 cm, 1 cm thick)

Step I

- Take the scrap cardboard, open it and roll it out.

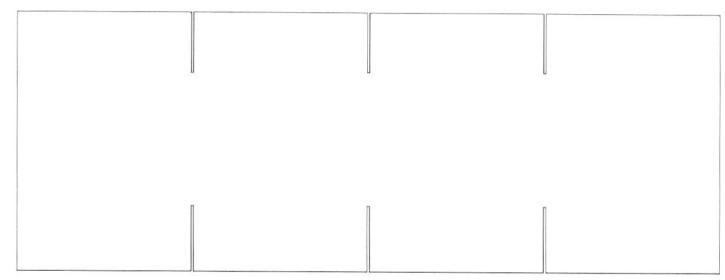

- With the paper tape, join the cuts from both sides of the cardboard.

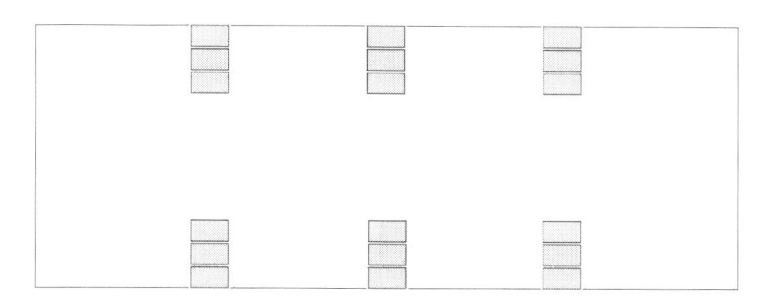

PAPER TAPE

- Measure the surface obtained.

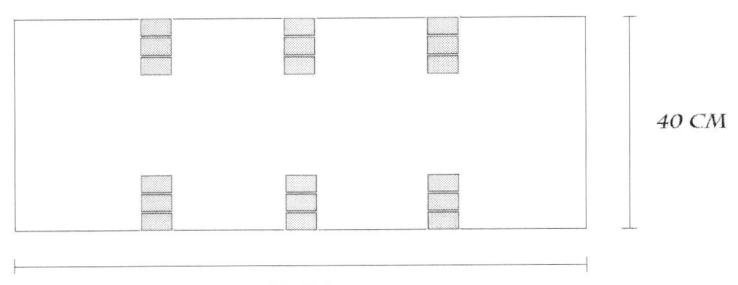

40 CM

55 CM

- If the cardboard sheet does not correspond to the measure needed for the front of the furniture (for instance 80cmx55cm), add another sheet of cardboard up to the desired size. Attach both sides of cardboard sheets with the paper tape.

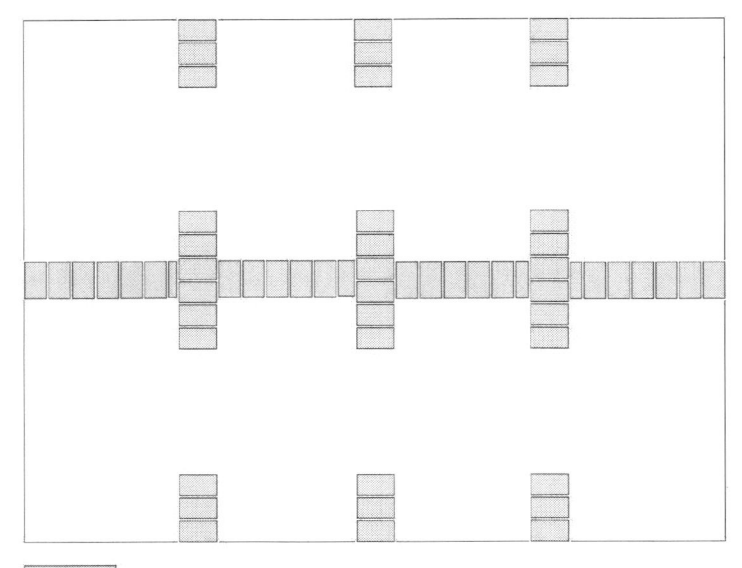

PAPER TAPE

Step II

Preparing the glue

- Pour 1 liter of water into a saucepan and add 200 gr. (7 oz.) of flour.
- Place the saucepan over a low flame, while stirring using the whisk pastry to obtain a uniform paste. This will occur after a few minutes.
- Continue the stirring until the flour does not stick to the bottom of the saucepan. Always check the density of the paste. When the consistency is similar to yogurt, remove the saucepan from the heat and continue the stirring for another minute.

- The glue is ready! Do not forget that you are using natural glue and therefore it cannot be used for long periods of time.

Step III

- Now you need a wooden surface, a brush, white newspaper sheets and glue.

- Take the regular-sized newspaper sheets and cut them in half, along the folded edge. Using smaller pieces, the paper is easy to manage and it does not stick to the wooden surface while working.

——— *CUT IT IN HALF, ALONG THE FOLDED EDGE*

- Place glue on the wooden surface using the paintbrush.
- Take one of the paper pieces and place it on the wooden surface making sure that no fold is made. This is a key point to ensure that glue covers the whole surface of the first sheet. Now, place glue on the surface of the sheet using the paintbrush. Once you do this, you may notice that the paper may be slightly folded. Do not worry about it as in this case, it won't have an impact on the quality of your work.

- Take a second white newspaper sheet and place it on the first sheet, adjust them in such a way that all four ends of the newspaper sheets are aligned (in the figure below they are not perfectly aligned so the reader can see the second sheet). Place glue on the whole surface of the second sheet.

- Take one more white newspaper sheet and place it on top of the second piece, ensuring that it is aligned with the previous sheets (in the picture below they are not perfectly aligned so the reader can see all the sheets). Place glue on the whole surface of the third sheet.

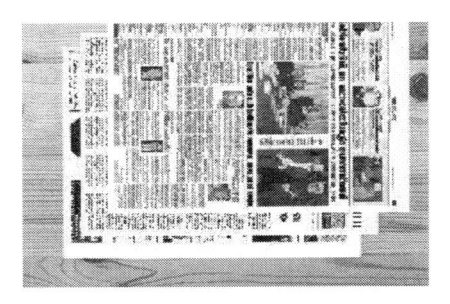

- Step III is now completed and the 3-layered white paper mâché is ready to be used. It is important to know that you can make paper mâché sheets with different layers. Remember:

More layers = more resistance and higher surface roughness,

Less layers = less resistance and less surface roughness, that is superior surface finish

Step IV

- Take a strip of 3-layered white paper mâché (of approximately 8 cm x 8 cm) and cover all the joints on both sides of the 80 cm x 55 cm cardboard sheet. Do not only cover the paper tape, but also apply the paper mâché strips to the adjacent areas on the cardboard. In this way, additional strength is built into the structure.

Sub-Step.1

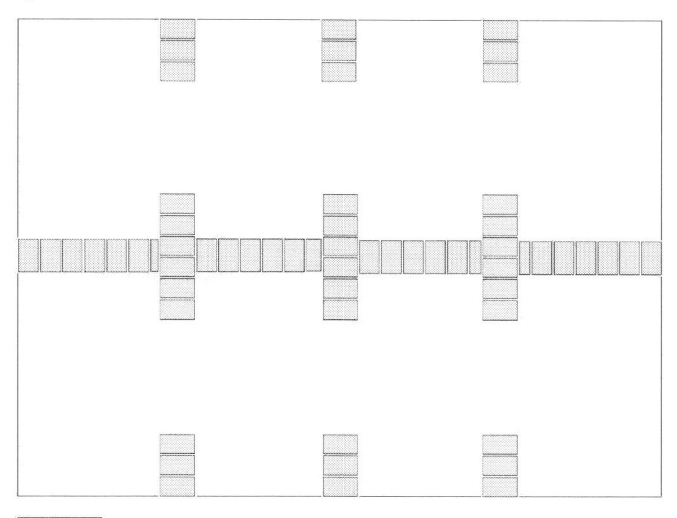

PAPER TAPE

Sub.Step.2

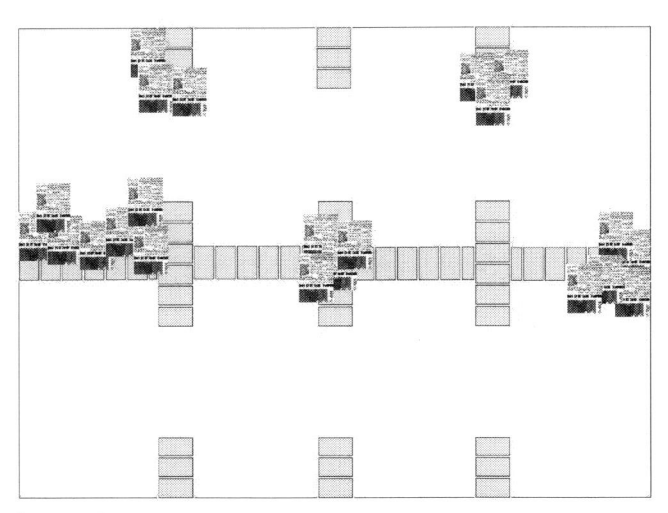

 PAPER TAPE

3-LAYERED PAPER MACHE STRIP (8cmx8cm)

Sub.Step.3

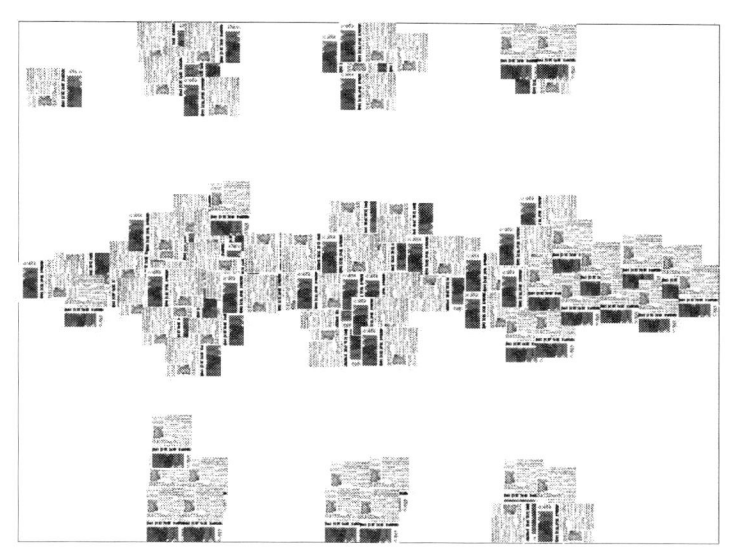

3-LAYERED PAPER MACHE STRIP (8cmx8cm)

• Once the first layer of white paper mâché is applied on all the joints, get the pink papers and create a 3-layered pink paper mâché sheet (if you do not remember how to create it, you may go to Step III).

• Take a strip of approximately 8cm x 8cm of 3-layered pink paper mâché and paste it on top of the white paper mâché on both sides of the 80 cm x 55 cm cardboard sheet.

Sub.Step.4

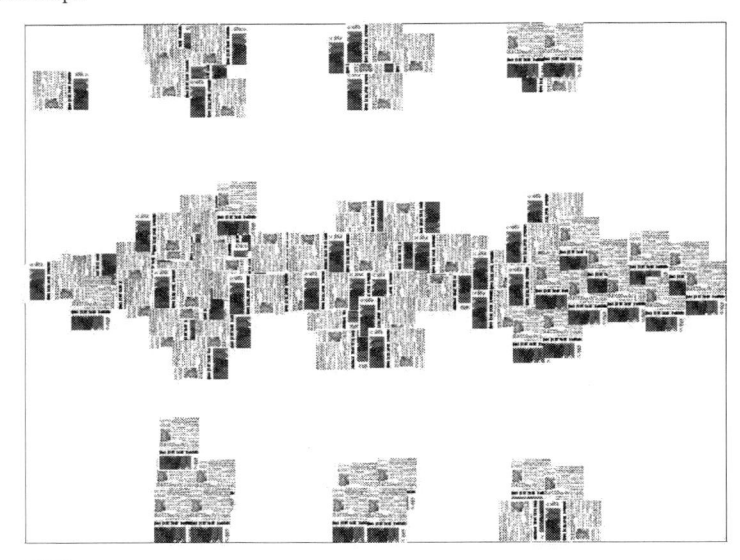

3-LAYERED PAPER MACHE STRIP (8cmx8cm)

Sub.Step.5

By now you have the following:

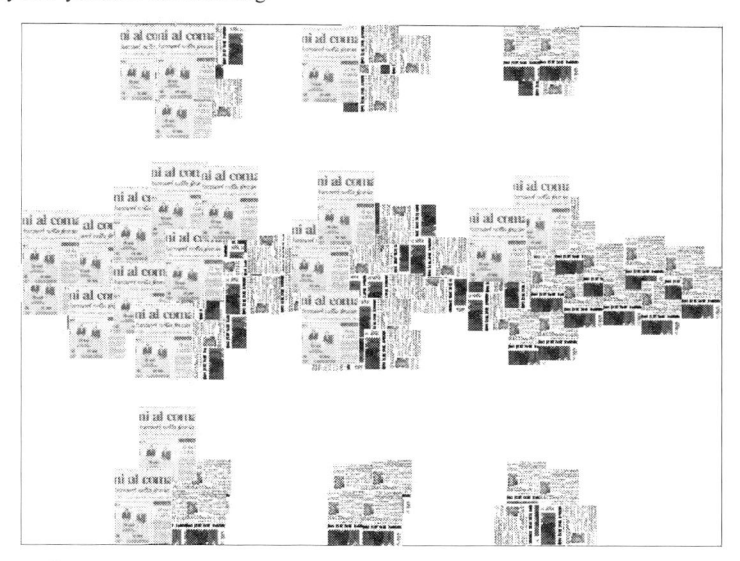

 3-LAYERED PAPER MACHE STRIP (8cmx8cm)

3-LAYERED PINK PAPER MACHE STRIP (8cmx8cm)

Sub.Step.6

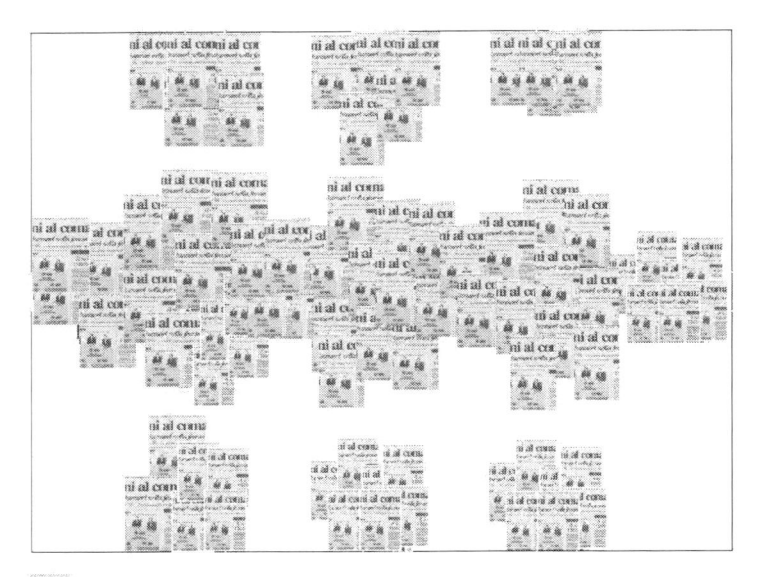

3-LAYERED PINK PAPER MACHE STRIP (8cmx8cm)

- Let the sheet dry for a day, preferably nearby a heat source. Congratulations! Now you have your first sheet of cardboard of 80 cm x 55 cm, 0.5 cm thick.

Step V

- Cardboard sheets of 80 cm x 55 cm and 1 cm of thickness are ideal if you want to create furniture of a remarkable stability. So if you want to build a solid structure you should have eight sheets of cardboard 80 cm x 55 cm 0.5 cm thick in total. Once you have these eight sheets of cardboard ready, go to Step VI.

Step VI

- Draw a grid on one of the eight cardboard sheets. It will allow you to faithfully reproduce the furniture of your project and to maintain symmetry.

GRID

- Draw the perimeter of the furniture to create its frontal part. Do not forget to mark the opening of drawers.

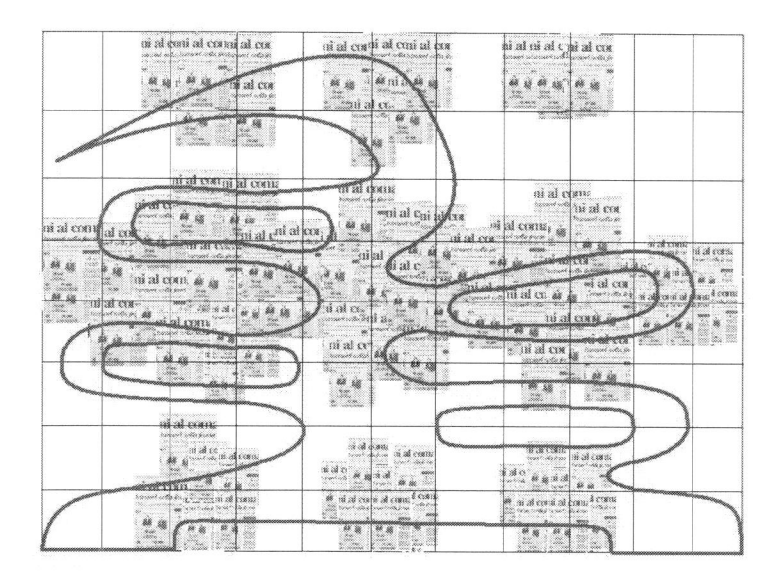

FURNITURE PERIMETER

Step VII

- Cut the cardboard all along the perimeter using a cutter.
- Once this step is completed, the first front part of the piece of furniture is done.

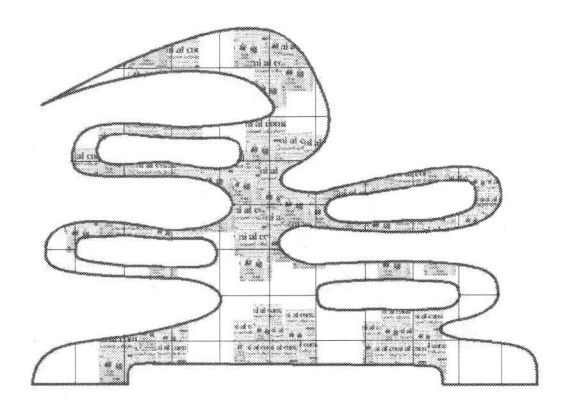

FRONT PART

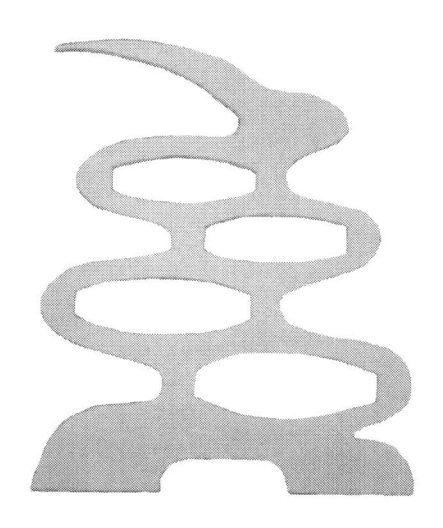

Step VIII

- Take the first frontal piece that you have just obtained and place it on the second cardboard sheet of 80 cm x 55 cm, 0.5 cm thick.

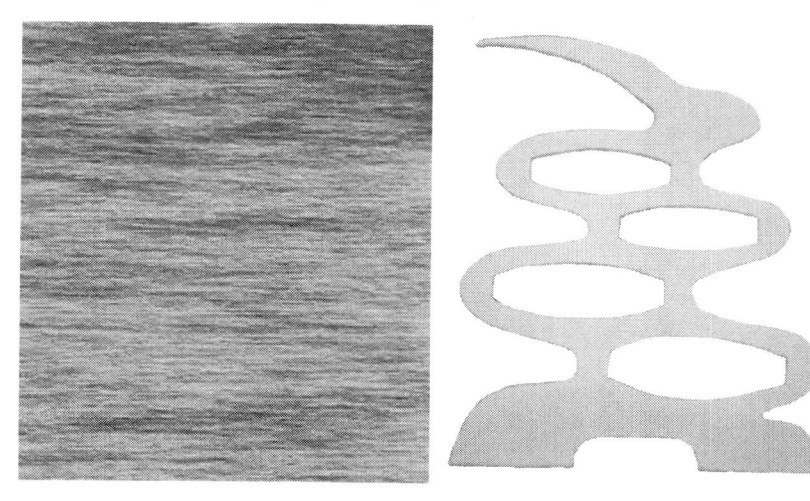

- Draw a line around the border of the shape in order to obtain the same shape on the second cardboard sheet.
- Once this is done, remove the first piece and cut the second design with a cutter.

- You got the second piece!

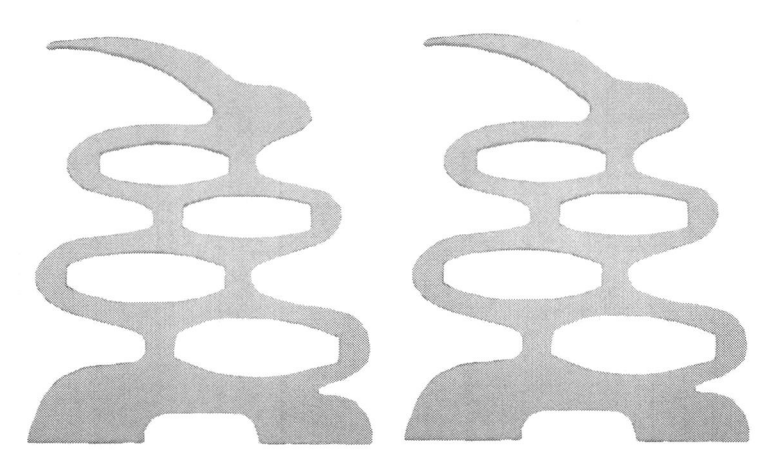

- Use the same technique until you make six identical pieces for the frontal view of furniture, including the respective holes for drawers.

Step IX

- Take again the first shape and place it on the seventh cardboard sheet (80 cm x 55 cm 0.5 cm thick)

 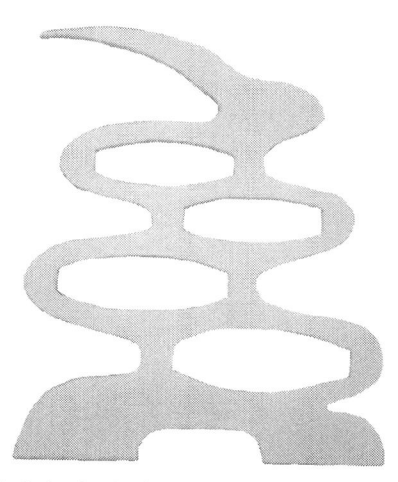

- Drawn with a pen the perimeter, avoiding the holes for the drawers, as this shape will be the back part of the furniture.
- Once you have drawn the perimeter cut it all around the line using a cutter.

- You got the seventh shape, the back piece.

- Repeat this process with the eighth cardboard sheet 80 cm x 55 cm, 0.5 cm thick in order to obtain the eighth shape, which will be part of the back too.

Step X

- At this point you should have six pieces with holes for the drawers and two pieces to be used for the back part of the furniture.
- Take the first piece with opening drawers and put a layer of glue on one of the surfaces, as it is showed below.

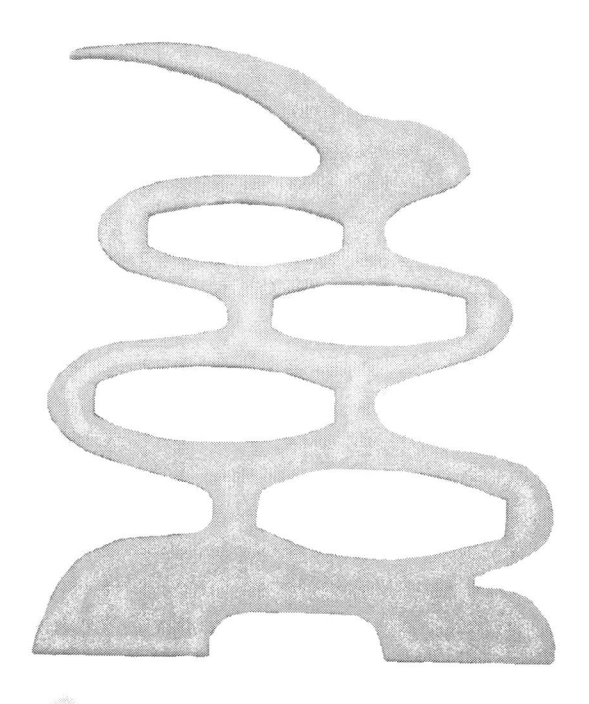

GLUE

- Then place it over a second identical piece so they can be glued together.

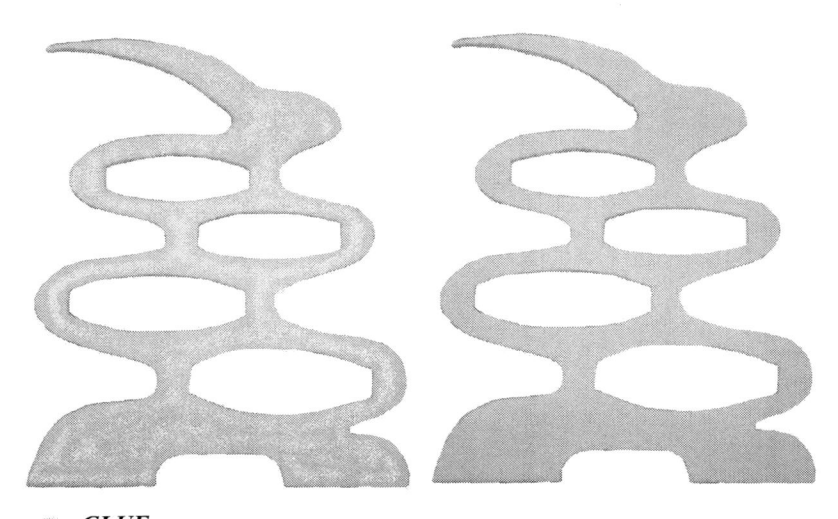

GLUE

- You should make sure that both perimeters match exactly.

- Perform the same steps in order to glue identical pieces in two as follows: the third + fourth pieces, the fifth + sixth pieces. And finally glue the seventh + eighth pieces with no holes together.
- Let them dry.
- At this point you got four double pieces of 80 cm x 55 cm, 1cm thick: Three pieces with openings for drawers and one without holes to be used for the back.

Step XI

- On the second and third pieces, perform small cuts of 2.5 cm x 0.8 cm. The amount of cuts in this example is 52.
- Be careful not to make cuts on weak points, where there is no much cardboard available.

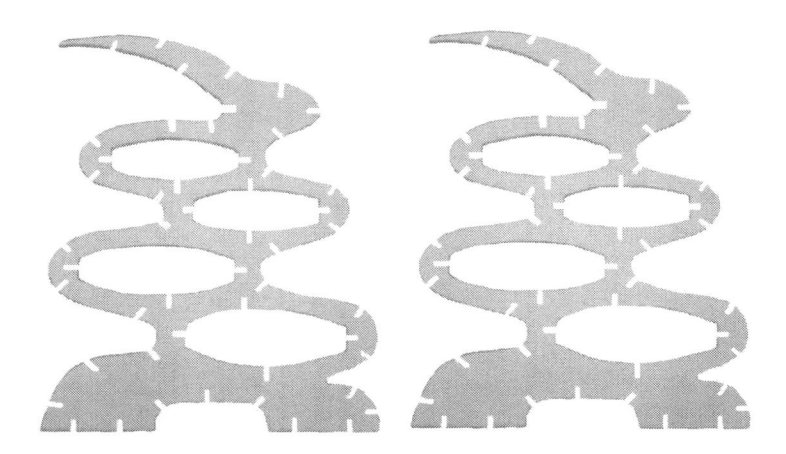

- Do NOT make any cut on the front and the back parts.

Step XII

- If you have done 52 cuts, you will need 52 rectangular cardboard pieces to be able to join all the furniture pieces together-
- As established during the design phase, the furniture will have a depth of 30 cm, so we are going to make the rectangular pieces with the following measures H. 5cm, L. 28cm, 1cm thick.
- If you do not have a cardboard sheet, take advantage of the technique detailed from Step I to Step V to make a cardboard sheet of 50 cm x150 cm, 1cm thick. From this sheet you can get 52 rectangular cardboard pieces.

- 9 cm away from the sides, you should make 2.5 cm x 0.8 cm cuts as detailed below:

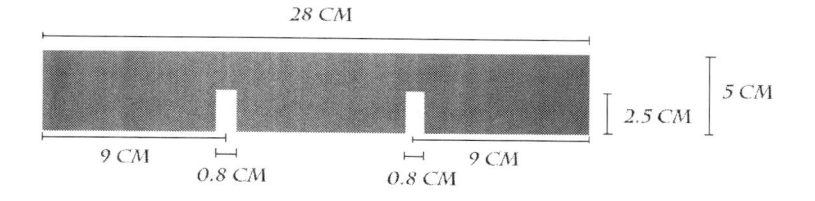

Step XIII

- Insert each of the rectangular pieces making sure that the cuts coincide so the second and third shapes are attached as it is showed in the next picture:

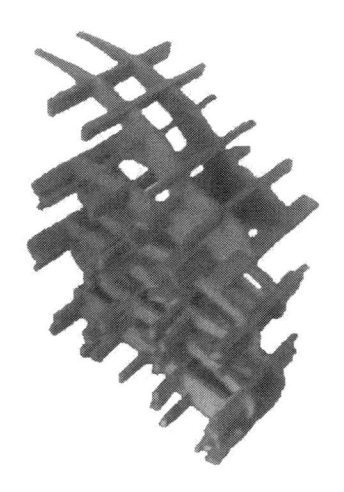

- Put some strips of 3-layered white paper mâché around each of the joints.

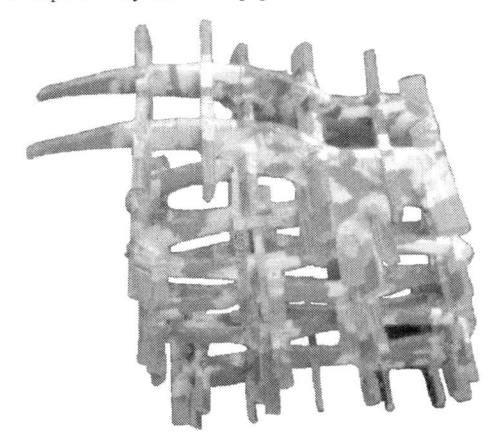

- Let the structure dry.

Step XIV

- Take the fourth piece (back) and place it on the table
- Now take the structure you have previously built and place the ends of the rectangular pieces on the back part.

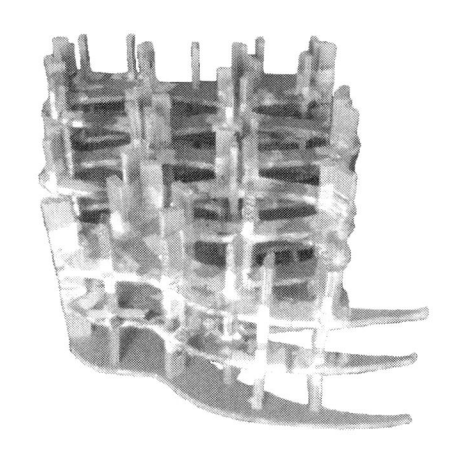

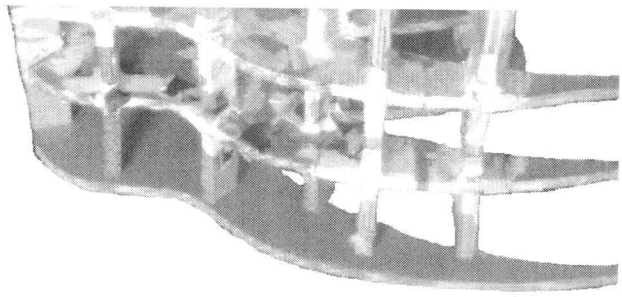

- Make sure that the perimeters of all the shapes are correctly placed. To do this you can use a setsquare or a level.

- Fix the ending part of the rectangular pieces to the fourth shape (back) with several strips of 3-layered white cardboard.

- Let the piece of furniture dry in this position

- Take the first piece (the front) and place it on the table.
- Take the second, third and fourth shapes that you joined together in Step XIV and place them on the front piece. Make sure that the rectangular pieces are within the perimeter.

- Check with a setsquare or a level that all the respective perimeters match.
- Fix the joints of the rectangular pieces with some strips of 3-layered white paper-mâché.

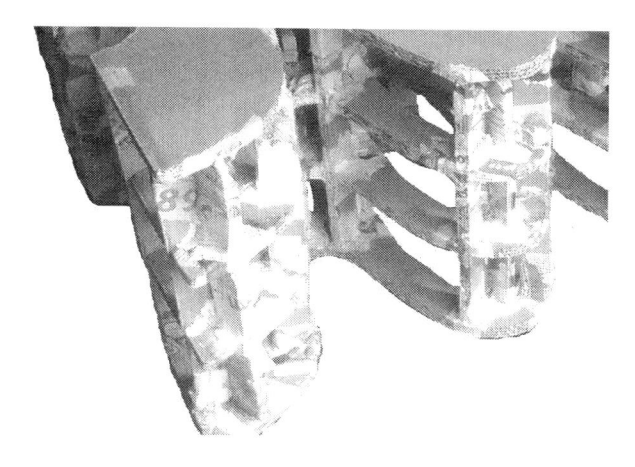

- Finally, let it dry

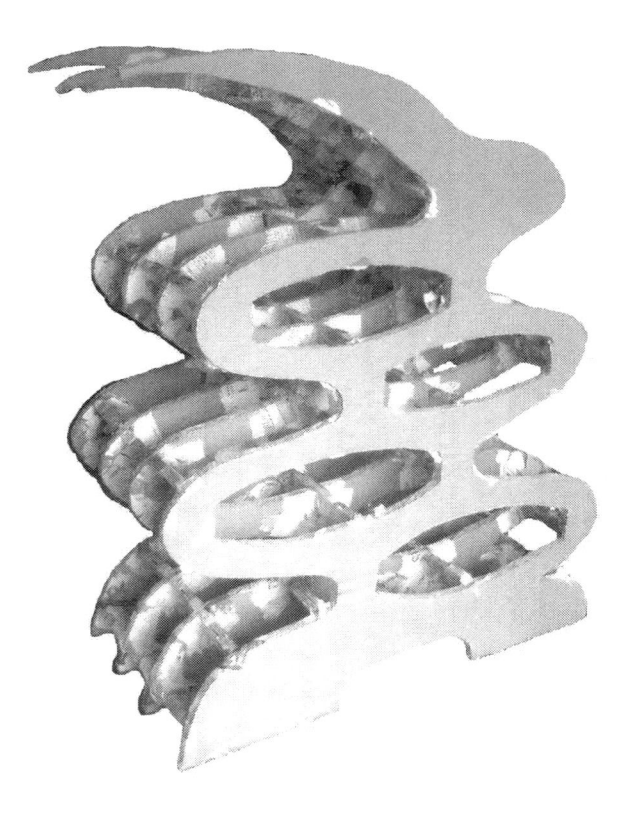

Step XVI

- Now it is turn for the drawers!
- Measure the inner perimeter using a tape measure
- Cut a piece of scrap cardboard 0.5 cm thick, which matches the drawer inner perimeter length and with a height of 29 cm.

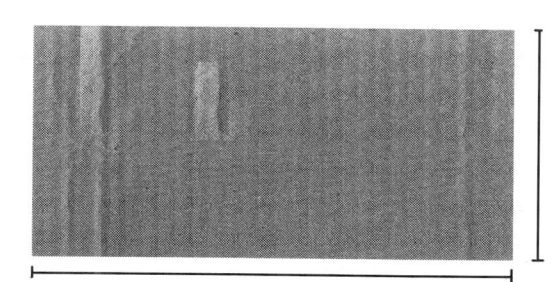

H. 29CM

L. = INNER PERIMETER OF DRAWER

- Fold the piece of cardboard you have just cut.

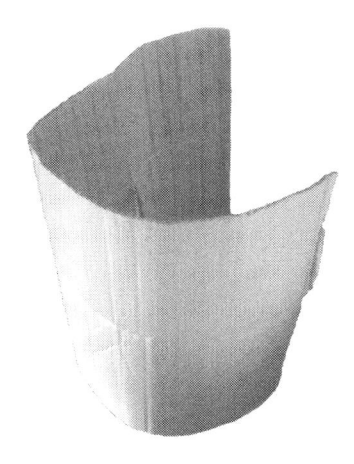

- Place the cardboard inside the drawer hole and secure it with paper tape. When you do so, you will notice that the perimeter of this piece is longer than the inner perimeter of the drawer.

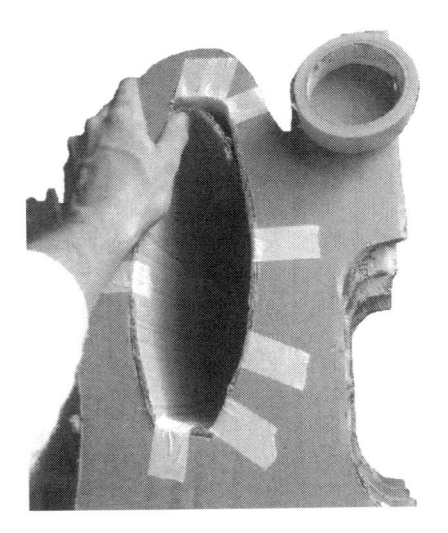

- Cut the surplus material.

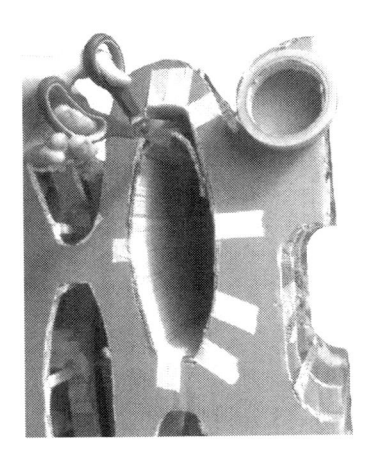

- Now, secure it with paper tape

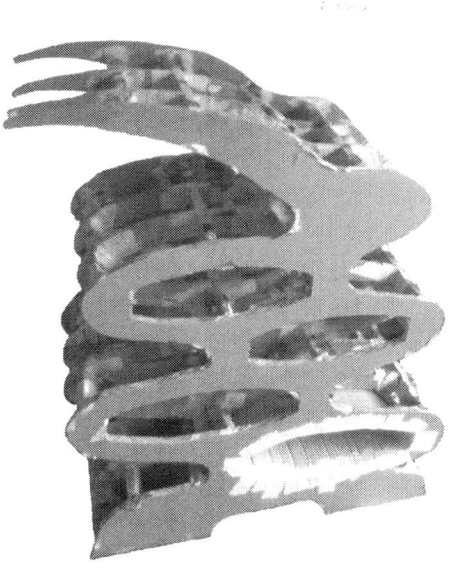

- Repeat the same process for each drawer

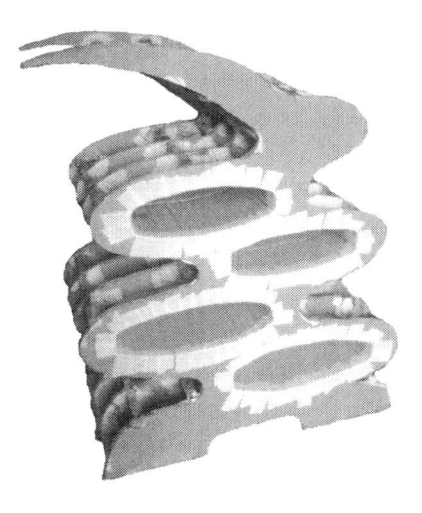

- Now, fix the pieces that you have just made using strips of white paper-mâché. Although the picture below is showed in a vertical position, it is important that during this process and the subsequent drying step, the structure remains in a horizontal position (on the back). In this way, detachment of the internal tray of the drawers can be avoided.

- Let it dry in horizontal position as mentioned before.

- Now place this piece along the perimeter of the furniture and hold it with tape.

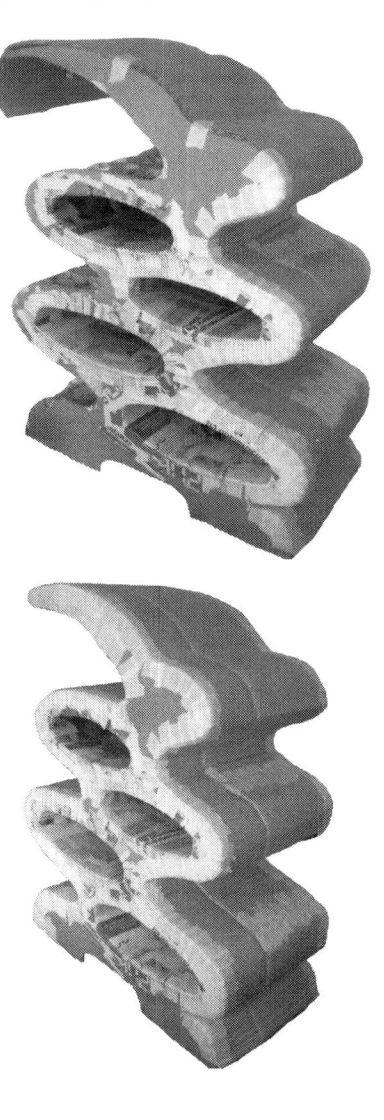

- Once the whole perimeter is fixed to the body of the piece of furniture, apply a layer of 3-layered white paper-mâché to the overall structure surface.
- Once this is done, apply another layer of 3-layered pink paper mâché to the surface.
- Finally, apply a layer of 2-layered white paper-mâché, making sure that the paper is perfectly glued to the surface and that no wrinkles are made.

- At this point the entire body of the piece of furniture is finished. Let it dry.

Step XIX

- Now we should focus on the drawers to complete the piece of furniture.
- Measure the internal perimeter of the drawer, excluding the top part.
- Take a piece of cardboard (0.5 cm thick) and fold it to get the shape of the drawer. The length of this piece should match the inner perimeter of the tray (excluding the upper perimeter), and its depth should be 29 cm. Fold the piece to get the desired shape and secure it with paper tape as it is shown in the figure.

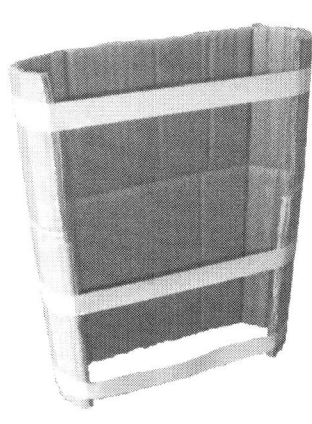

- Now prepare the back part of the drawer by cutting a sheet of cardboard 0.5 cm thick, so it can be adapted to the size and shape of the drawer.

- Now fix it with paper tape to the other piece of the drawer.

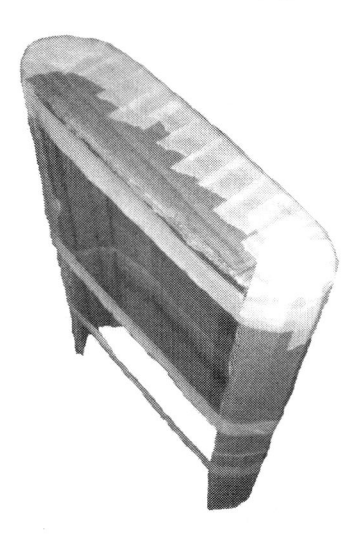

- It is time to decide the shape of the front part. To offer more resistance a cardboard of 1 cm thick should be used.

- Once you have cut it, fix this piece to the previously assembled components with paper tape.

- Try placing the drawer in its compartment to make sure it fits and it is possible to open it easily.

- Now you just need to cover the drawer with two layers of 3-layered paper mâché.

- Once dried, try the drawer into its compartment. If the drawer does not open easily, you can remove some imperfections using sandpaper.

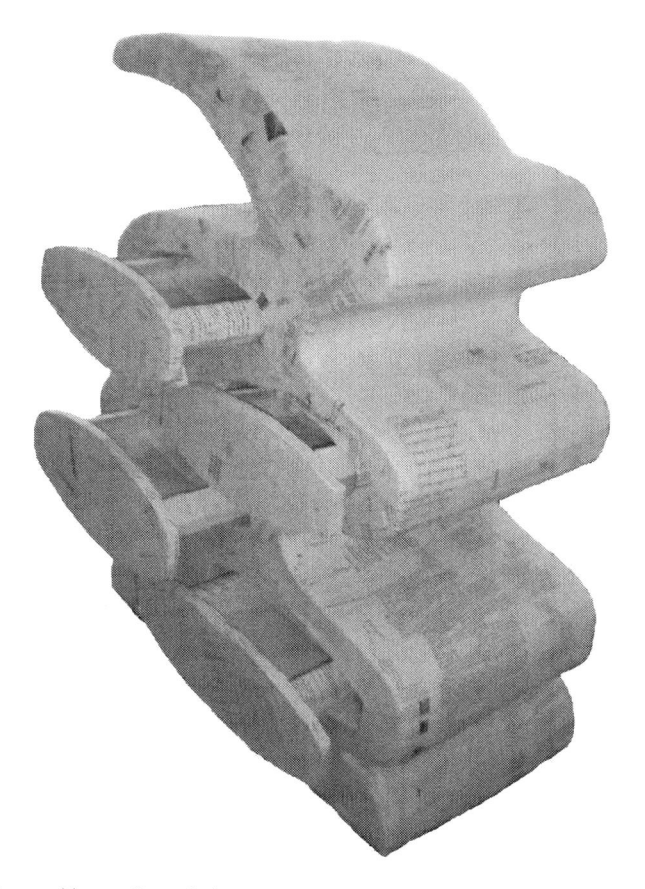

- Repeat this step for each drawer.

Step XX

- Your piece of furniture is finished!
- Use the sandpaper over the entire structure in order to make the surface smooth.
- Paint the overall structure using white paint (the one used to paint the walls). Once it is dry, apply a second coat of white paint.
- Let it dry. Now it is time to move on… to color! Use your imagination!

- Let the paint dry. Give a coat of water based wood varnish, no colored, to the furniture. At this point be careful not to push the brush too much on the colored parts, to avoid removing the colors.
- Let the varnish dry. Give a second coat to the overall structure. This time you do not need to worry about removing the colors behind as the first varnish coat protects them.
- Clean the brush with turpentine

Congratulations! You have made your first cardboard piece of furniture!

Color Table

Some tips on how to use primary colors to get the color pallete for your furniture are described in this section.

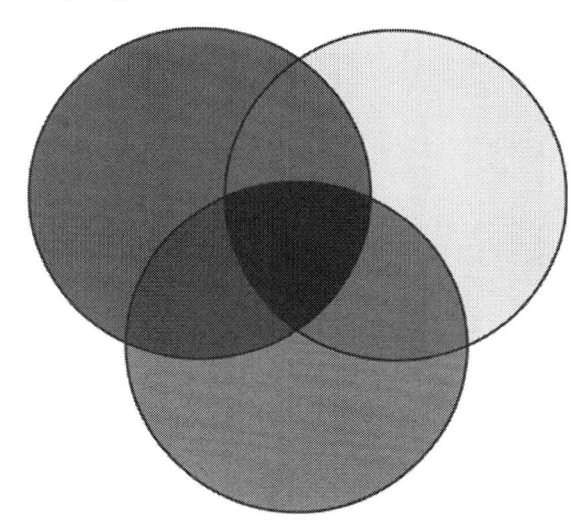

By mixing the primary colors in equal parts, secondary colors are obtained:

- orange (red + yellow)
- green (yellow + blue)
- purple (blue + red)

When mixing primary colors, different hints of colors can be obtained depending on the amount of paint is added. Therefore, I suggest that you buy the following colors: red, yellow, blue and black acrylic water colors, while you can use the paint used for walls for the white color.
I invite you to try and have fun mixing colors to get the shades you desire.

Conclusions
I hope this book is useful to learn techniques, tips and tricks but also to allow you create cardboard furniture.
Now that you know my secrets I invite you to dream and create incredible furniture. Design, create and have fun.

Acknowledgments
To Gabriella, Domitilla and Ana who hold me every time I fall down. To "babbo Filippo" who is looking at me from a star.

Un musicista deve fare musica, un pittore deve dipingere, un poeta deve scrivere, se vogliono essere veramente in pace con se stessi.

A musician should make music, a painter should paint, a poet should compose poetry if they really want to be at peace with themselves.

Thank you!
Riccardo Agostini

adamo1978@yahoo.it

Content

Printed in Great Britain
by Amazon